GRATITUDE

Meditations
& Inspirations

GRATITUDE
is the sign of
NOBLE SOULS.

—AESOP

GRATITUDE

Meditations & Inspirations

MANDALA

AMAZING
how we light
tomorrow with
TODAY.

—ELIZABETH BARRETT BROWNING

JOY
is the simplest form of
GRATITUDE.

—KARL BARTH

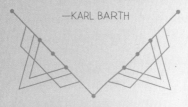

I think that real friendship always makes us feel such sweet gratitude, because the world almost always seems like a very hard desert, and the flowers that grow there seem to grow against such high odds.

—STEPHEN KING

I'm thankful for each and
EVERY DAY.
We never know when
TIME IS UP.

—CHUCK BERRY

THANKFULNESS

may consist
merely of words.

GRATITUDE

is shown in acts.

—HENRI-FRÉDÉRIC AMIEL

Henceforth I ask not good

FORTUNE

—I myself am good fortune.

—WALT WHITMAN

GRATITUDE is a powerful catalyst for HAPPINESS. It's the spark that LIGHTS A FIRE of joy in your soul.

—AMY COLLETTE

"Thank you" is the best prayer that anyone could say. I say that one a lot. Thank you expresses extreme gratitude, humility, understanding.

—ALICE WALKER

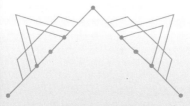

HOW glad I am that
YOU EXIST.

—VITA SACKVILLE-WEST

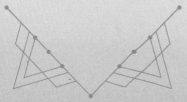

I've always believed in

SAVORING

the moments.

IN THE END,

they are the only things

WE'LL HAVE.

—ANNA GODBERSEN

GRATITUDE
is not only the
GREATEST
of virtues, but the
PARENT OF
all the others.

—CICERO

Good morning. Lead with

GRATITUDE.

The air in your lungs, the sky

ABOVE YOU.

Proceed from there.

—LIN-MANUEL MIRANDA

GRATITUDE
doesn't change the
scenery. It merely
WASHES CLEAN
the glass you look through
so you can clearly see
THE COLORS.

—RICHELLE E. GOODRICH

what makes me

HAPPY

is the appreciation of

PEOPLE

around me.

—NADIA COMANECI

Be thankful for what
you have; you'll end
up having more.
If you concentrate on
what you don't have,
you will never, ever
have enough.

—OPRAH WINFREY

GRATITUDE
makes sense of our
PAST,
brings peace for
TODAY,
and creates a vision for
TOMORROW.

—MELODY BEATTIE

we should learn to

SAVOR

some moments to let

TIME

feel worth existing.

—MUNIA KHAN

Maybe being grateful
means recognizing
what you have for
what it is. Appreciating
small victories. Admiring
the struggle it takes to
simply be human.

—SHONDA RHIMES

The mutual practice of
GIVING
and receiving is an
EVERYDAY
ritual when we know
TRUE LOVE.

—BELL HOOKS

LOVE
casts out fear, and
GRATITUDE
can conquer pride.

—LOUISA MAY ALCOTT

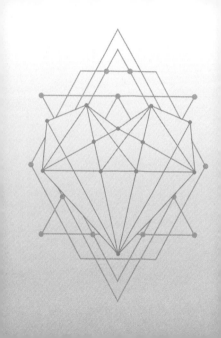

Happiness cannot be
traveled, owned, earned,
worn, or consumed. Happiness
is the spiritual
experience of living
every minute with love,
grace, and gratitude.

—DENIS WAITLEY

unless you're completely

EXPLODED,

there's always

SOMETHING

to be grateful for.

—SAUL BELLOW

what you truly acknowledge truly is yours. invite your heart to be grateful and your *thank you*'s will be heard even when you don't use words.

—PAVITHRA MEHTA

the world is full of

MAGIC
THINGS,

patiently waiting for

our senses to

GROW
SHARPER.

—WILLIAM BUTLER YEATS

If you are really

THANKFUL,

what do you do?

YOU SHARE.

—W. CLEMENT STONE

GRATITUDE

is more of a compliment to

YOURSELF

than someone else.

—RAHEEL FAROOQ

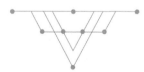

appreciation, not

POSSESSION,

makes a thing ours.

—MARTY RUBIN

BE about ten times more

MAGNANIMOUS

than you believe

YOURSELF

capable of.

—CHERYL STRAYED

the trick is to be

GRATEFUL

when your mood

is high and

GRACEFUL

when it is low.

—RICHARD CARLSON

reflect upon your present blessings, of which every man has plenty; not on your past misfortunes, of which all men have some.

—CHARLES DICKENS

Open your
heart to the sky.
LIVE.

—ADAM GNADE

TO SPEAK
gratitude is courteous
and pleasant,
TO ENACT
gratitude is generous
and noble, but
TO LIVE
gratitude is to
touch Heaven.

—JOHANNES GAERTNER

Just do the next

RIGHT THING,

and be grateful for the

CHANCE

you have to go do that.

—ROGER EBERT

GRATITUDE

is a duty which ought
to be paid, but which
none have a right to

EXPECT.

—JEAN-JACQUES ROUSSEAU

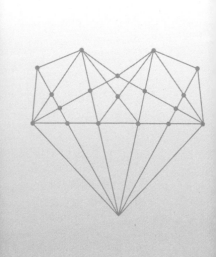

A sense of blessedness
comes from a change
of heart, not from
more blessings.

—MASON COOLEY

BLESSED

are those who can

GIVE

without remembering and

TAKE

without forgetting.

—BERNARD MELTZER

when you rise in the morning, give thanks for the light, for your life, for your strength. give thanks for your food and for the joy of living. if you see no reason to give thanks, the fault lies in yourself.

—TECUMSEH

RECEIVING

is harder than giving . . .
but gifts are made to be

ACCEPTED.

—DANI HARPER

Any chance you have to

SEE THE
WORLD

through someone else's
eyes is always a

GIFT.

It allows you to live your
own life more clearly.

—FOREST WHITAKER

There are only two ways to
live your life. one is as though

NOTHING IS
A MIRACLE.

The other is as though

EVERYTHING
IS A MIRACLE.

—ALBERT EINSTEIN

SAVOR
with me the lushness of a
LINGERING
sleep . . . and last night's
DREAM.

—SANOBER KHAN

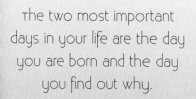

the two most important
days in your life are the day
you are born and the day
you find out why.

—MARK TWAIN

the root of joy is

GRATEFULNESS.

—DAVID STEINDL-RAST

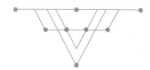

WAKE
at dawn with a winged heart and

GIVE THANKS
for another day of loving.

—KHALIL GIBRAN

enjoy the
LITTLE THINGS,
for one day you may
LOOK BACK
and realize they were the
BIG THINGS.

—ROBERT BRAULT

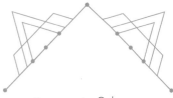

I'm grateful we
GET AWAY WITH
as much as we do.

—SETH MACFARLANE

The more one does and sees and feels, the more one is able to do, and the more genuine may be one's appreciation of fundamental things like home, and love, and understanding companionship.

—AMELIA EARHART

NO man knows until he has

SUFFERED

from the night how

SWEET

and dear to his

HEART

and eye the morning can be.

—BRAM STOKER

i want to taste the glory
in each day, and never be
afraid to experience pain.

—SYLVIA PLATH

GRATITUDE

also opens your eyes to
the limitless potential of
the

UNIVERSE,

while dissatisfaction
closes your eyes to it.

—STEPHEN RICHARDS

That I can read and be
HAPPY
while I am reading, is a great
BLESSING.

—ANTHONY TROLLOPE

I'm so thankful for

FRIENDSHIP.

It beautifies life so much.

—L. M. MONTGOMERY

I'm not sorry for
wanting what I
DESERVE
and I'm not afraid
to walk away to
FIND IT.

—r.h. SIN

i will no longer

COMPARE

my path to others.

I REFUSE

to do a disservice to

MY LIFE.

—rupi kaur

NO matter how bad things are, you can at least

BE HAPPY

that you woke up this

MORNING.

—D. L. HUGHLEY

I don't have to chase
extraordinary moments
to find happiness—
it's right in front of me if
I'm paying attention and
practicing gratitude.

—BRENÉ BROWN

the newness
of this day is
DIVINE.

—LAILAH GIFTY AKITA

Ingratitude is

MONSTROUS.

—WILLIAM SHAKESPEARE

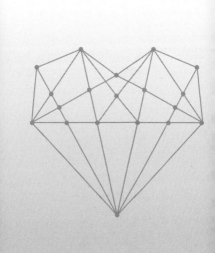

The essence of all
BEAUTIFUL
art, all great art, is
GRATITUDE.

—FRIEDRICH NIETZSCHE

PLAY
the hand you're
DEALT.

—JAWAHARLAL NEHRU

The mind is like a flower.
It does not bloom without
the lights of appreciation,
encouragement, and love.

—DEBASISH MRIDHA

we often take for
GRANTED
the very things that
most deserve our
GRATITUDE.

—CYNTHIA OZICK

It takes a great deal of

COURAGE

to see the world in all its

tainted glory, and still

LOVE IT.

—OSCAR WILDE

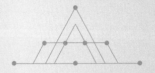

I make the most of all
that comes and the
least of all that goes.

—SARA TEASDALE

my socks may not
MATCH,
but my feet are always
WARM.

—MAUREEN MCCULLOUGH

not what we say about our

BLESSINGS,

but how we use them,

is the true measure of our

THANKSGIVING.

—W. T. PURKISER

But to pay
ATTENTION
is to love
EVERYTHING.

—SARAH MANGUSO

some people

GRUMBLE

that roses have

THORNS;

I am grateful that

thorns have

ROSES.

—ALPHONSE KARR

savor the mystery
. . . we don't get
enough of them.

—DAVID MCCALLUM

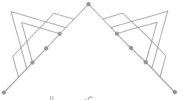

walk as if you are

KISSING

the earth with your feet.

—THÍCH NHẤT HANH

the more
GRATEFUL
i am, the more
BEAUTY
i see.

—MARY DAVIS

you never know what
worse luck your bad luck
has saved you from.

—CORMAC MCCARTHY

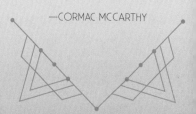

KINDNESS

can only be repaid with
kindness. It can't be

REPAID

with expressions
like "Thank you."

—MALALA YOUSAFZAI

rest and be

THANKFUL.

—WILLIAM WORDSWORTH

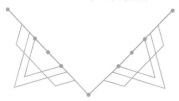

It is wonderful to be grateful. To have that gratitude well out from deep within you and pour out in waves. Once you truly experience this, you will never want to give it up.

—SRIKUMAR RAO

GRATITUDE

unlocks all that's blocking
us from really feeling

TRUTHFUL,

really feeling authentic
and vulnerable and

HAPPY.

—GABRIELLE BERNSTEIN

we should certainly
count our blessings, but
we should also make
our blessings count.

—NEAL A. MAXWELL

gratitude is a
CURRENCY
that we can mint for
ourselves, and spend
WITHOUT
fear of bankruptcy.

—FRED DE WITT VAN AMBURGH

The human heart beats approximately 4,000 times per hour and each pulse, each throb, each palpitation is a trophy engraved with the words "You are still alive."

you are still alive.

ACT LIKE IT.

—RUDY FRANCISCO

I regard the gift of
admiration as indispensable
if one is to amount to
something; I don't know where
I would be without it.

—THOMAS MANN

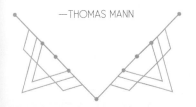

THANKS

are the highest form of

THOUGHT;

and that gratitude is

HAPPINESS

doubled by wonder.

—G. K. CHESTERTON

The world is three days:
As for yesterday, it has
vanished along with
all that was in it. As for
tomorrow, you may
never see it. As for today,
it is yours, so work on it.

—HASAN OF BASRA

gratitude is the
WINE
for the soul. go on.
GET DRUNK.

—RUMI

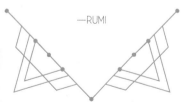

There is a
CALMNESS
to a life lived in
GRATITUDE,
a quiet joy.

—RALPH H. BLUM

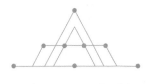

what a wonderful
LIFE I'VE HAD!
I only wish I'd realized it
SOONER.

—SIDONIE-GABRIELLE COLETTE

The only
PEOPLE
with whom you
should try to
GET EVEN
are those who have
HELPED YOU.

—JOHN E. SOUTHARD

I hear the wind blow,
and I feel that it was
worth being born just
to hear the wind blow.

—FERNANDO PESSOA

SILENT
gratitude isn't
very much to
ANYONE.

—GERTRUDE STEIN

I used the
doors that were

SHOWN

to me, and a lot
of them saved

MY LIFE.

—SAMUEL L. JACKSON

AS WE EXPRESS our gratitude, we must NEVER FORGET that the highest APPRECIATION is not to utter words but to LIVE BY THEM.

—JOHN F. KENNEDY

At some point in life,
the world's beauty
becomes enough.

—TONI MORRISON

There are always

FLOWERS

for those who want to

SEE THEM.

—HENRI MATISSE

I may not be where
I WANT TO BE
but I'm thankful for
not being where
I USED TO BE.

—HABEEB AKANDE

Don't cry
because it's over.

SMILE

because it happened.

—DR. SEUSS

gratitude is when
MEMORY
is stored in the
HEART
and not in the mind.

—LIONEL HAMPTON

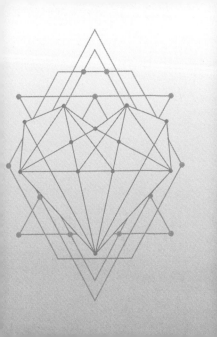

As each day comes to us

REFRESHED

and anew, so does my

GRATITUDE

renew itself daily.

—TERRI GUILLEMETS

I savor life. When you have anything that threatens life . . . it prods you into stepping back and really appreciating the value of life and taking from it what you can.

—SONIA SOTOMAYOR

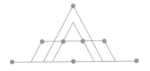

TO GREET
a lovely morning, we
MUST LEAVE
the night behind.

—TARANG SINHA

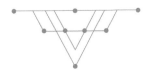

NO one is as capable of

GRATITUDE

as one who has

EMERGED

from the kingdom of

NIGHT.

—ELIE WIESEL

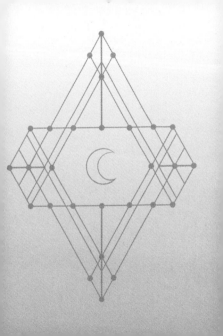

Being thankful is not

ALWAYS

experienced as a

NATURAL

state of existence, we must

WORK AT IT,

akin to a type of

STRENGTH

training for the heart.

—LARISSA GOMEZ

we are cups,
constantly and quietly
BEING FILLED.
the trick is knowing how to
tip ourselves over and let the
BEAUTIFUL
stuff out.

—RAY BRADBURY

Someone

I LOVED

once gave me a box full of

DARKNESS.

It took me years to

UNDERSTAND

that this, too, was a gift.

—MARY OLIVER

Every morning,

I WAKE UP

and think about ten

different things I'm

THANKFUL

for. I continue to spread

that love throughout

THE DAY.

Always visualizing,

meditating, and

GROWING.

—SHAMEIK MOORE

Enjoy your

ACHIEVEMENTS

as well as your plans.

—MAX EHRMANN

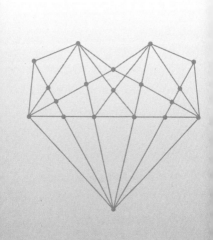

HOW LUCKY
I am to have something
THAT MAKES
saying goodbye so hard.

—A. A. MILNE

The moment of
PERCEIVING
something beautiful
CONFERS
on the perceiver the
GIFT OF LIFE.

—ELAINE SCARRY

Life is not a series of
PROBLEMS
to be solved, it's a
JOURNEY
that you should be
fascinated by.

—BRIANNA WIEST

I adore my own
LOST BEING,
my imperfect substance, my
SILVER SET,
and my eternal loss.

—PABLO NERUDA

GRATITUDE looks to the
PAST and love to the
PRESENT; fear, avarice, lust,
and ambition look ahead.

—C. S. LEWIS

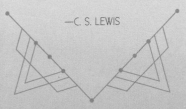

Life is not
MEASURED
by the number of
BREATHS
we take, but by the
MOMENTS
that take our breath away.

—MAYA ANGELOU

never forget how to
BE A KID
and never let the magic,
MYSTIQUE,
and mystery of the
WORLD
stop amazing you.

—GLORIA ATANMO

The real voyage of
discovery consists not in
seeking new landscapes
but in having new eyes.

—MARCEL PROUST

GRATITUDE

is the sweetest thing in a

SEEKER'S LIFE

—in all human life.

—SRI CHINMOY

there's a special
place in my

HEART

for the ones who
were with me at my

LOWEST

and still loved me
when I wasn't very

LOVABLE.

—YASMIN MOGAHED

A simple expression of

THANKFULNESS

can go a long way in

RELATIONSHIPS

and communication with

OTHERS.

—DANIELLA WHYTE

Two kinds of gratitude:

the sudden kind
WE FEEL
for what we take;
THE LARGER
kind we feel for what
WE GIVE.

—EDWIN ARLINGTON ROBINSON

GRATITUDE
is a quality similar to
ELECTRICITY;
it must be produced and
DISCHARGED
and used up in order to
EXIST AT ALL.

—WILLIAM FAULKNER

APPRECIATION

is a wonderful thing:

It makes what is

EXCELLENT

in others belong

to us as well.

—VOLTAIRE

IN LIFE,
one has a choice to
take one of two paths:
TO WAIT
for some special day or to
CELEBRATE
each special day.

—RASHEED OGUNLARU

CHALLENGES
are what make life
INTERESTING
and overcoming them
is what makes life
MEANINGFUL.

—JOSHUA J. MARINE

FEELING
gratitude and not
EXPRESSING
it is like wrapping a
PRESENT
and not giving it.

—WILLIAM ARTHUR WARD

Appreciation can make a
day, even change a life.
Your willingness to put
it into words is all that is
necessary.

—MARGARET COUSINS

if we had no

WINTER,

the spring would not be so

PLEASANT.

—ANNE BRADSTREET

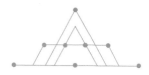

New beginnings are often

DISGUISED

as painful endings.

—LAOZI

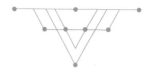

There are no

MENIAL

jobs, only menial

ATTITUDES.

—WILLIAM JOHN BENNETT

Stop now.

ENJOY

the moment.

IT'S NOW

or never.

—MAXIME LAGACÉ

we create
OURSELVES
by what we
CHOOSE
to notice.

—MARGARET WHEATLEY

there is no

FEAR

for one whose

MIND

is not filled with

DESIRES.

—THE BUDDHA

Hardship is a blessing when it spurs effort and development; ease is a curse when it increases complacency and self-indulgence.

—MUSO KOKUSHI

The highest
TRIBUTE
to the dead is not
GRIEF
but gratitude.

—THORNTON WILDER

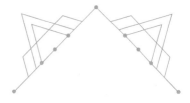

Find the good and
PRAISE IT.

—ALEX HALEY

May the
GRATITUDE
in my heart kiss all the
UNIVERSE.

—HAFEZ

Let all your thinks be

THANKS.

—W. H. AUDEN

what do i think of
when i look at the sky?

JOY.
GRATITUDE.
LOVE.

—YOKO ONO

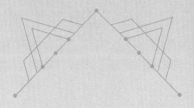

My day begins and ends with

GRATITUDE.

—LOUISE HAY

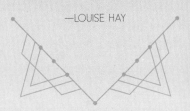

cultivate the habit of
being grateful for every
good thing that comes
to you, and to give
thanks continuously.
And because all things
have contributed to
your advancement, you
should include all things
in your gratitude.

—RALPH WALDO EMERSON

you can give without

LOVING,

but you cannot

love without

GIVING.

—AMY CARMICHAEL

the soul that gives

THANKS

can find comfort in

EVERYTHING;

the soul that

COMPLAINS

can find comfort in

NOTHING.

—HANNAH WHITALL SMITH

make choices that bring love and joy to your body. It's not about perfection; it's about love and gratitude for an amazing body that works hard and deserves your respect.

—ALYSIA REINER

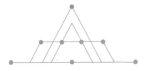

the best way
to pay for a lovely

MOMENT

is to enjoy it.

—RICHARD BACH

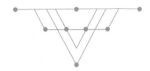

GIVING

is an expression of

GRATITUDE

for our blessings.

—LAURA ARRILLAGA-ANDREESSEN

An early morning walk is a

BLESSING

for the whole day.

—HENRY DAVID THOREAU

stop thinking of

GRATITUDE

as a byproduct of your

CIRCUMSTANCES

and start thinking of it as a

WORLDVIEW.

—BRYAN ROBLES

when life is

SWEET,

say thank you and

CELEBRATE.

and when life is

BITTER,

say thank you and

GROW.

—SHAUNA NIEQUIST

SHOWING gratitude is one of the SIMPLEST yet most powerful things HUMANS can do for each other.

—RANDY PAUSCH

WHATEVER you are doing, love YOURSELF for doing it. whatever you are FEELING, love yourself for feeling it.

—THADDEUS GOLAS

when we focus on our

GRATITUDE,

the tide of disappointment

GOES OUT,

and the tide of love

RUSHES IN.

—KRISTIN ARMSTRONG

I believed that days
would be too full forever,
too crowded with friends
there was no time to see
. . . I was wrong.

—JOAN DIDION

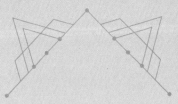

THANKFULNESS

is the quickest

PATH TO JOY.

—JEFFERSON BETHKE

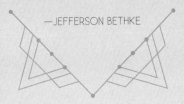

DARKNESS
must fall before we
ARE AWARE
of the majesty of
THE STARS
above our heads.

—STEFAN ZWEIG

Saying
THANK YOU
is more than
GOOD MANNERS.
It is good
SPIRITUALITY.

—ALFRED PAINTER

MANDALA

Mandala Publishing
PO Box 3088
San Rafael, CA 94912
www.MandalaEarth.com

Find us on Facebook: www.facebook.com/MandalaEarth

Follow us on Twitter: @mandalaearth

Follow us on Instagram: @mandalaearth

978-1-68383-975-0

Manufactured in China by Insight Editions

10 9 8 7 6 5 4 3 2

2021 2022 2023